# More than a Pretty Face

## Empowering Women to Love and Value Their Inner Beauty

LaShone L. Grimes

authorHOUSE®

*AuthorHouse™*
*1663 Liberty Drive*
*Bloomington, IN 47403*
*www.authorhouse.com*
*Phone: 1 (800) 839-8640*

*Published by AuthorHouse 10/23/2018*

*ISBN: 978-1-5462-6370-8 (sc)*
*ISBN: 978-1-5462-6368-5 (hc)*
*ISBN: 978-1-5462-6369-2 (e)*

*Library of Congress Control Number: 2018912164*

For family and friends who have encouraged me to turn my obstacles into opportunities to succeed

# ACKNOWLEDGMENTS

Sensitivity, encouraging words, hope, diligence, and motivation are all attributes that my family has shown throughout my venture of writing this book. Thank you for standing by my side to see my dream come true. It would not have happened without your undying support.

# Contents

# AUTHOR'S MESSAGE

"The Beauty of a Woman"

The beauty of a woman
Isn't in the clothes she wears,
The figure that she carries,
Or the way she combs her hair.

The beauty of a woman
Must be seen from in her eyes
Because that's the doorway to her heart
The place where love resides.
—Maya Angelou

This poem speaks to the heart of why I wrote this book. It depicts a woman who values and loves her inner beauty. Many times we forget that outer beauty is temporal but inner beauty lasts forever. Billboards advertising beauty products, runway model queens, and this pretty-face society have diluted the truth about valuing inner beauty. Have you ever wondered why beauty commercials focus only on developing a woman's appearance? Why aren't there commercials for products to help us enhance our *inner* beauty? Developing character, having self-confidence, and setting goals are also important.

You were created to be more than a pretty face. Your talents, abilities, dreams, aspirations, goals, and strengths are all inside of you. Accept the daily challenge to develop and enhance these vital attributes lurking inside you. My deepest hope is that this book sparks your determination to value and love your *inner beauty*! Be strong, confident, and motivated to be your best at whatever you do. And remember that you were created for a purpose, designed for greatness, and destined for success!

# INTRODUCTION

Welcome into the world of a compassionate, confident, and self-motivated woman. Born on April 28, 1972, in Savannah, Georgia, I weighed a healthy seven pounds and five ounces. My parents, Elliot Lamar Sams and Bessie Lee Sams, welcomed their beautiful daughter, who was destined for greatness, created for a purpose, and designed for excellence.

Now let's begin the journey into LaShone's life. Huge oak trees with gray moss, cobblestone sidewalks, and splendid front porches are all part of southern life in Savannah. As a child, I wondered why our trees were covered with that grayish stuff called Spanish moss, which was especially scary at night. My imagination would run wild, and I thought it looked like gigantic spiders in a web. But as I grew older, my thoughts about Spanish moss changed drastically. At thirteen, I finally began to appreciate the serene beauty of this seaport city.

As an only child for several years, I grew up in a loving and nurturing home. My precious and wise maternal grandparents, Verdell and Elouise Samuels, were positive role models who imparted significant values in my life. Elouise Samuels, known as Grandma Ella, was a wise woman who loved the Lord and exemplified self-confidence, self-respect, and determination. Married at a young age, she migrated with my grandfather to Savannah from Estill, South Carolina, with fifty cents in her pocket. Grandma Ella gave me many lectures about finishing school and getting a good education. She often told me, "Baby, get good marks in school and get your education. Don't allow your circumstances to stop you from pursuing anything in life. Work hard and never give up." When Grandma Ella said, "Get good marks," that meant to get good grades. I endeavored each school year to abide by those words of wisdom.

Grandma Ella was also a strong believer in being her own boss. She had a strong niche in the real estate business and enjoyed being a successful businesswoman. She and my grandfather owned several lucrative pieces of property in Savannah, and they worked diligently to build their business. At a young age, I saw how they worked together as a team to make their lives successful.

With this strong woman by his side, Grandpa Verdell was also a pillar of strength for our close-knit family. A short, small-framed man with a huge heart, Grandpa Verdell worked hard, persevered diligently, and displayed great confidence every day of his life. He loved icy cold Coca-Cola, and he would give his last dollar—or even the shirt off his back—to anyone who needed it. Yes, his giving heart was the essence of his being. By watching him handle difficult situations with care and wisdom, I learned how to be confident in myself and maintain a high level of determination. Grandpa Verdell never buckled under life's pressures, but persevered until his goals were reached.

A host of other people helped mold and shape this shy, quiet little girl. My dad, Elliot Lamar Sams, was a wonderful father. Even though my parents divorced when I was two years old, my daddy was always an active part of my life. He crowned me with a special nickname, Pookie, which is still used in my family. I like it when my daddy calls me Pookie, because it brings back precious memories of when I was a young girl. Daddy instilled in me the lifelong values of self-confidence and respect for myself and others. He taught me to be more than a pretty face. As a little girl, I watched him walk with proud confidence and speak with grace. His unique sense of humor can make the angriest man, woman, or child chuckle with laughter. Daddy loves a good chuckle and seeing other people laugh with joy.

As I reminisce about my precious childhood, I remember how my father and I spent time together on weekends. He would take me to birthday parties and the park on Saturdays. That was exciting because I got an opportunity to have fun with friends and just be a kid. Dad was an ordained minister at Asbury United Methodist Church in Savannah, so Sundays were church time for us. Dad taught me that going to church and having a special relationship with God was vitally important. After church, Daddy and I would eat delicious dinners and take quiet, peaceful walks on the beach.

For summer vacation, Daddy would take me to Cave Springs, Georgia, the home of my paternal grandparents, Charles and Eleanor Sams. Granddaddy Charles, known as Papa Sams, was a tall, slender man who always had a sweet smile on his face. His beautiful gray eyes lit up any room and he spoke with a deep southern voice. Grandma Eleanor was known around Cave Springs as Mama Sams, but in my mind, she was Mama Chef. I believed that her cooking skills exceeded those of anyone in the entire country. Mama Sams's meals could make your toes curl, and every weekend their home was filled with relatives and friends who loved her scrumptious dinners.

Papa and Mama Sams would always admonish me to speak positively and confidently. They frequently reminded me that it's easy to speak negatively, but it takes greater energy to talk about positive things. Mama Sams would encourage me to say positive words about myself or others. Their rich belief that your words shape your world was evident each time they spoke to me. They also taught me that hard work is necessary for success and that nothing comes easy for anyone. Success comes at a price and the willingness to sacrifice something.

Who else has shaped the mind and character of LaShone? My phenomenal mother, Bessie Lee Ferguson, raised her daughter to be more than a pretty face. Throughout my childhood, I witnessed her undying strength, courage, and determination. This strong and confident lady taught me the value of being the best at whatever I endeavored to do in life. She always reminded me to never settle for second best. Her words of wisdom still echo in my mind: "Be the best. Pursue the best. Never accept anything less!" My mother never ceased to amaze me with her diligence, perseverance, and determination to be successful.

My mother was an educator for thirty years, and I saw how strong and confident she was on a daily basis. I never heard her say "I can't" or "I don't think we're going to make it," and she always had an encouraging word for me. I learned at a young age, by observing my mother persevere against any odds, to have a "stick to it" attitude. She became a single parent when I was two years old, but I never saw her give up or back down from any challenge. Wow, what an awesome woman. Now in her seventies, she still is confident in herself, believes in hard work, and never utters the words "I can't."

Many influential women such as my mother, Bathsheba Sams, Eleanor Williams, and Sandra Font encouraged me to be more than a pretty face. I learned early that although my outer beauty might eventually fade, my inner beauty would transcend my external being. Long eyelashes, naturally curly hair, full lips, a perfect narrow nose, thick thighs, and pretty legs are not the *only* attributes we have as women. We need to realize that our inner beauty can be developed into something beautiful. Accept the challenge to build your inner beauty, which is a treasure chest filled with self-confidence, determination, motivation, self-respect, diligence, perseverance, and intelligence.

Building inner beauty takes hard work, commitment, and dedication. For many years, we have focused our attention on beautifying our external facades. Of course, there is nothing wrong with caring about your appearance, but don't let that be your only focus. Cultivate and build what's inside you. Take the time and initiative to rebuild the low self-esteem that might be lurking inside. Accept the challenge to be self-confident about who you are and your purpose in life. Speak positively to yourself daily and remind yourself that you are unique, special, created for a purpose, destined for greatness, and designed for excellence.

# CHAPTER ONE

## A Reflection of Me

Make the most of yourself, for that is all there is of you.

—Ralph Waldo Emerson

Ladies, marrying at eighteen years old and having my first child caused me to examine myself and reflect on who I saw in the mirror. With little experience of how to be a good wife and mother, I had to look deep within myself to evaluate who I was. As I tried to adjust to motherhood and marriage, I would frequently question myself:

- Can I accomplish my goals with the added responsibility of a baby?
- Do I have the self-confidence to complete college?

- Am I willing to make sacrifices to accomplish my goals?
- Do I have the ability to be a good wife to my husband?

These questions haunted me every day as I persevered to complete my college education. Numerous times I wanted to give up and throw in the towel, but I remembered what my grandparents, parents, and husband always told me: "If you want something bad enough, you'll work for it." These inspiring words of motivation kept my dreams alive and caused me to persevere each day, and it was worth all the sacrifice and struggle.

Every woman has a mirror that shows her reflection. The history of mirrors starts in the third century BC. From ancient times, special qualities had been given to mirrors that no other object in the world had. The Greek philosopher Socrates gave advice to young men to look at themselves in the mirror. He said those who were handsome should focus their lives on keeping their souls clean and staying away from the temptations that could take them on the wrong path (InvitingHome.com).

As you look at yourself daily, what do you see? Does your reflection reveal …

- a woman who was sexually abused as a child?
- a woman with many insecurities about her appearance?
- a woman who has been emotionally scarred by men in relationships?
- a woman afraid to love her husband?
- a woman who views her mistakes as failures or windows of opportunities?
- a woman who is strong and intelligent?
- a woman who is determined to succeed despite challenging circumstances?

Whatever your reflection shows, it will shape how you think. The things that you think about yourself will determine your destiny in life. God says in Philippians 4:8, "And now, dear brothers and sisters, one final thing. Fix your thoughts on what is true, and honorable, and right, and pure, and lovely, and admirable. Think about things that are excellent and worthy of praise."

Once upon a time, there was a young lady who refused to look at herself in a mirror, even though every day her parents and sisters encouraged her to do so. She believed that if she looked at herself, she would see mistakes, failures, disappointments, and hurts. After much encouragement by her family, she finally agreed. As she stepped in front of the mirror, nervous and fearful, she saw something beautiful! More than just a pretty face, she saw a person who was intelligent, smart, strong willed, honest, responsible, self-centered, insecure at times, lazy, a gossiper, compassionate, shy, a risk taker, trustworthy, and a procrastinator. She saw attributes she liked and disliked about herself.

An honest look at the *real* you makes you want to step back and say, "Whoa, is this really me? Am I really this type of person?" It might not all be pretty, but the areas that aren't pretty can be developed into something beautiful. Change takes time—it never happens overnight. A butterfly isn't beautiful until it goes through several stages of metamorphosis.

- Stage 1 is the egg development process. Butterfly eggs have a hard outer shell that protects the larvae inside. The shell inside is called the chorion. Inside, the egg is lined with wax that keeps the egg from drying out.
- Stage 2 is when larvae develop with three body parts: head, thorax, and abdomen. Larvae have a set of real legs and five false legs called prolegs.
- Stage 3 is the process when the larvae pupate. They split the exoskeleton and the larval skin comes off. When the skin is partially off, the cremaster appears. That's the spiny part at the end of the abdomen from which the baby butterfly hangs until it is strong enough to fly.
- Stage 4 is the adult stage in which the butterfly has six legs with three body parts: head, thorax, and abdomen. It develops a proboscis, which is a long, straw-like tongue used for sucking up nectar and water. The caterpillar has now developed into a beautiful butterfly that escapes from its cocoon to fly, fly, fly.

Just as you take journeys to develop and rebuild those areas of your life that aren't especially pretty, you can fly to success. Will your flight to success get tedious, bumpy, and rough? Yes, my friend, it will. The more success you desire, the tougher the flight will be, but nothing comes easy to those who want more success out of life. The price of success is hard work, diligence, patience, endurance, perseverance, dedication, commitment, and self-motivation. My friend, don't be afraid to pay the price. It's worth it!

**Words of Reflection:** Success comes in cans, not can'ts. —Author unknown

Do you value yourself? *Webster's Ninth New Collegiate Dictionary* defines *value* as a "rate or scale in usefulness, importance, or general worth." Every woman should value herself. Regardless of what people say about you, it is your responsibility to realize that you have a valuable and important purpose on this earth. Your value is not determined by acceptance from others, economic background, or financial status. Valuing yourself comes from your internal being. It happens because you have decided to see and appreciate your usefulness and importance to society. Learn to appreciate your uniqueness, talents, and abilities. Realize that no one else is just like you. Do you believe that you were created for greatness and designed for a special purpose? Accept the challenge to be your best!

Once upon a time, an old bag lady walked the streets of her city every day. She struggled to survive, never knowing where her next morsel of bread would come from. Every night, she would curl into a damp, chilly corner and wish she could find the strength to *value* herself. Through the years, she had allowed mistakes and failures to shatter her sense of self-worth. Troublesome marriages, alcohol problems, and a cocaine addiction had engulfed her. One day as she walked through a familiar neighborhood, she reminisced about being a child and the joy of riding bikes with friends, picking plums from the plum tree, and playing kickball in her best friend's backyard. As she passed a green house with white shutters, she saw an elderly, gray-haired woman sitting quietly on her porch.

When the elderly woman noticed the bag lady, she approached the fence and asked, "Are you my student who always won the spelling bees in class and believed she was the smartest girl in school? I don't remember your name, but I vividly remember your face."

The bag lady replied, "Yes, I'm your student from third grade, but I've grown old and ugly. I've been through several divorces, lost my home, and squandered all my money on cocaine. In my younger years, I stood tall, held my head high, and was proud of my accomplishments. But I've allowed hard times to zap my ability to value myself."

The elderly woman took the bag lady by the hand and said, "Honey, no matter what tough times you go through, never lose the ability to value yourself. First, you must believe in yourself. Change what you think and say about yourself, and then you'll value yourself again."

Upon hearing these words, the bag lady began to cry. But after a moment, she looked at her wise third-grade teacher with confidence and said, "I accept the challenge of regaining my ability to value myself. Never again will I allow my circumstances to hinder my sense of self-worth. This day, I promise to believe in myself and think and speak with confidence." Then she gave the old woman a hug and walked away.

Three years later, the bag lady's former teacher was sitting in her kitchen reading the newspaper. On the first page was a photo of an older woman wearing a blue suit and a fancy white hat. The headline read, "You Are Never Too Old to Pursue Your Dreams." The former teacher recognized the face, but not the name. The article described how the bag lady had faced struggles in life but finally reached a crossroads. Her need to value herself and regain her sense of self-worth had ignited a lifelong dream to establish a homeless shelter for women with drug addiction(s). Suddenly, the teacher exclaimed, "Oh my, this is my third-grade student with whom I talked three years ago." Happy tears streamed down her face as she remembered wisely advising her former student to regain the ability to value herself.

This familiar story shows how women can come to a point in their lives where they begin to *devalue* themselves because of past mistakes, failures, and disappointments. As a young mother and wife, there were times when I devalued myself and allowed hardships to shatter my self-worth. I would ask myself, "Did I make a mistake by marrying so young and having a daughter?" However, I used these three steps to regain my ability to value myself:

1. Believing in yourself is vitally important. No one can believe in you if you don't first believe in yourself. Feel confident about your unique abilities, talents, and gifts. Appreciate who you are and make any necessary changes to become a better person.

**Self-Strength Quote**: I believe in myself. I am unique, special, and determined to succeed. I am full of confidence, strength, and determination. This is who I am. I am designed for greatness and created for a purpose!

2. Think with confidence, which requires you to see yourself as successful. Your thinking can determine your success, so stop the negative stinkin' thinkin'. When you begin to think confidently, you will speak with confidence. Think good things about yourself and view yourself as self-motivated, responsible, and intelligent.

**Self-Strength Quote:** I think with confidence. I am full of motivation and strength to excel beyond my obstacles. What I think about myself determines my greatness and success. What I think about myself determines how I reach my goals. My mind is set to think the best about myself!

3. Speak with confidence, because the words that you speak can determine your destiny. Constantly saying negative things about yourself will cause you to doubt yourself and hinder your ability to accomplish your goals. However, speaking positive words about yourself will strengthen your self-confidence. Your words can build you up or tear you down.

**Self-Strength Quote:** The words I speak will shape my world. I will speak with confidence and pride, always striving to be and do my best. I will never doubt myself, because I believe that I can pursue my dreams, achieve my goals, and reach success!

**Words of Reflection:** People are like stained-glass windows. They sparkle and shine when the sun is out, but when the darkness sets in, their true beauty is revealed only if there is light from within. —Elisabeth Kubler-Ross

## Where Are Your Hidden Talents and Abilities?

When I was a child, my mother always encouraged me to do my best in my academic career. My teachers and parents knew that I had a special talent for writing, which came easy for me. I always knew there were books inside me that needed to be written to encourage women to value their inner beauty. I promised myself each year that I would start writing, but I never put any actions into my words—until now. First I had to do a self-examination and search within myself for my hidden talents.

Cemeteries are filled with people who died without ever discovering their own hidden talents and abilities. Many women have left this earth without having reached their full potential, never knowing that they could have owned a lucrative business, won a Nobel Peace Prize, or discovered the cure for a disease. Don't let this happen to you. Take advantage of opportunities that come your way. Seize the moment to accomplish your goals and fulfill your destiny. Find your own buried talents and abilities, and then develop and strengthen them.

*Webster's Ninth New Collegiate Dictionary* defines a talent as a "natural endowment of a person." Some people have a talent for interior design, and others are successful entrepreneurs. Whatever your talent is, use and develop it. *Webster's* defines an ability as "the physical, mental, or legal power to perform." A women's ability to play basketball or to establish an organization can remain concealed, but it's your responsibility to develop your abilities. Sometimes we neglect our abilities, especially if past failures make us want to push them into a dungeon and leave them there. Unveil your abilities and let each one come forth!

My daughters, Alexia, Trinity, and Victoria, have a natural ability to play basketball, which was developed at a young age. My husband took valuable time and energy to help them develop this ability with year-round basketball camps, intense practice times, and summer tournaments. Sometimes it may take another person to point out those abilities buried within you.

## Identifying My Strengths and Weaknesses

Here's a simple exercise to help identify your strengths and weaknesses. Get two sheets of paper and write *My Strengths* on one sheet and *My Weaknesses* on the other. When writing your strengths and weaknesses, be honest with yourself. When both sheets are complete, evaluate your list of weaknesses and make an action plan to improve in those areas. Weaknesses are areas in your life that need work and development, so set goals to improve in those areas by following these three important steps:

- Make an honest decision to change the areas that need work, such as procrastination or unreliability.
- Set short- and long-term goals for improvement. For example, if one of your weaknesses is that you don't eat healthful meals, make an itemized grocery list with healthful food items that need to be part of your diet. Discipline yourself and purchase only those items on the list.
- Realize that progress might take time. Rome was not built in a single day. Neither will you overcome your weaknesses in one day or perhaps in three weeks. Traits and habits take a tremendous amount of time to become ingrained. Be very aggressive in your goals but be realistic as well.

Evaluating yourself requires you to analyze your past failures and use them as learning tools, but your major strengths must also be considered. As you analyze your strengths, create ways to maintain and strengthen them. For example, if you have strong interpersonal skills, join civic clubs and community organizations to enhance those skills.

**Words of Reflection:** What lies behind us and what lies before us are tiny matters compared to what lies within us. —Anonymous

# CHAPTER TWO

# Seeing Success for Yourself

The men who try to do something and fail are infinitely better than those who try to do nothing and succeed.

—Lloyd Jones

Success. What does this familiar seven-letter word mean to you? When someone says the word *success*, what influential person comes to your mind? Do you believe that success happens overnight, or does it take time? Is success only for those who have grown up with financial wealth or pursued higher education? Or maybe success requires hard work, diligence, and determination. Whatever your ideology may be, success requires you to believe in yourself, work hard, and take positive risks. It is vitally important to envision success for yourself and then dedicate your energy, effort, and determination to making that vision a reality. Women must realize that we can successfully accomplish our dreams and aspirations. Open your mind and begin to understand the hidden success that lies dormant within your inner being. Because of past failures and mistakes, sometimes we place lids on our goals and aspirations and then they die, but we have a major responsibility to ourselves to remove those lids. Pursue your hidden dreams and achieve whatever your life's destiny.

Phenomenal women such as Madam C. J. Walker, Shirley Chisholm, and Mary Kenney O'Sullivan took the lids off their dreams and became huge successes. Madam C. J. Walker was an African American woman who became a pioneer in the hair and cosmetics industry during the twentieth century. Her unwillingness to limit her dreams was evident in how she became the first female millionaire. Having amassed a fortune in fifteen years, she had a prescription for success— perseverance, hard work, faith in herself and God, honest business dealings, and producing high-quality products. Walker once said, "There is no royal flower strewn path to success. And if there is, I have not found it—for if I have accomplished anything in life, it is because I have been willing to work hard."

Shirley Chisholm, the oldest of four girls born to parents who immigrated from the West Indies, became the first African American woman elected to the US Congress and the first to campaign for the presidency. This catalyst for diversity and change said, "I know I will survive. I'm a fighter." Yes, indeed she was a strong warrior who saw success for herself and possessed a non - quitting attitude!

Another success giant was Mary Kenney O'Sullivan, the first female salaried organizer for the American Federation of Labor. Her diligence and determination helped the organization for garment workers, printers, carpet weavers, and show workers. Focusing on the women's suffrage movement, she worked diligently to promote protective legislation such as establishing a minimum wage and trade unionism among women.

These strong, proud women envisioned success for themselves and didn't allow anything to prevent them from pursuing their dreams and accomplishing their goals. More than just pretty faces, they were vessels of strength, self-confidence, and determination.

## Success Is a Process

Many people—Barack Obama, Michelle Obama, Maya Angelou, Bill Gates, Oprah Winfrey, and so on—become phenomenally successful. Their determination to never give up makes them *success giants* in their particular field, but success doesn't occur overnight. It requires years of hard work, diligence, and perseverance. Sometimes we want success to happen quickly, but it's a process.

One of my favorite activities during Christmas holidays is baking red velvet cakes. Does a delicious cake just magically appear on my dinner table? No, it requires following a set of precise directions. First, cake flour and baking soda are combined. Then butter, milk, egg, and sugar are added. Finally vanilla flavoring and red food coloring are added and the cake batter is poured into two round cake pans. In an oven heated to 350 degrees, the cake is baked for an hour and a half. Is baking a red velvet cake a process? Yes, my friend, it is.

Success, too, requires journeying through a specific and diligent process. If people desire success, they must be willing to persevere. Several crucial steps can aid in your journey to achieving success:

First, believe in yourself. Otherwise it's impossible for anyone else to believe in you. Believe in your talents and abilities, and be confident in who you are and your purpose in life.

Second, write an action plan. Start by buying a spiral notebook and write one specific goal that you want to accomplish at the top of the first page. Then jot down *how* you're going to accomplish that goal. For example, if your goal is to start a small bakery business, write that at the top of the page. Underneath that goal, write how it will be accomplished. To open a small bakery, you might start by (1) creating a business plan, (2) taking a few business courses, and (3) applying for a business license. These are simple examples of how you're going to achieve the goal.

Third, put your action plan to work. As the saying goes, "Actions speak louder than words." Put your action plan to work, and you'll start to see results over a period of time.

Fourth, evaluate your action plan. Evaluation time is *never* lost time, because it allows you to identify areas that need improvement. For example, if your business plan needs more detail about marketing strategies, then diligently seek help from an expert in marketing. Success is a process that requires people to persevere despite challenging circumstances. Determination, hard work, and commitment are significant attributes that all assist in leaping onto a path of success.

## Can Your Failures Be Windows of Opportunity for Success?

You can either use your failures to strengthen your character or view them as obstacles. If you want to strengthen your character, you can learn from failure, sharpen your skills, develop them into even greater attributes, and move forward. Many successful and influential people failed before they reached success. The inventor Thomas Edison was a pioneer in the use of electricity, but it took numerous attempts before he produced a successful electric light bulb. Despite his early failures, Edison pressed forward through numerous trials, never giving up.

If you view failure as an obstacle, difficult challenges in life become impossible to overcome. Your self-confidence is shattered and you doubt the potential that lies within you. Positive thoughts about your purpose in life dwindle and failure is used as an excuse to *not* move forward. Goals become burdensome and your focus wavers. Ultimately, life becomes a constant rat race, rather than an opportunity to excel and succeed.

However, failures can become windows of opportunity. A failure is simply an unexpected event that requires you to evaluate yourself and the circumstances that led to the disappointment. Never allow failures to deter you from accomplishing your goals. Failures don't determine your destiny, but how you *handle* failure will determine your future success.

There was a specific time in my life that helped me understand that failures do not control my destiny. When I decided to pursue a master's degree in public administration at Savannah State University, I needed to take the entrance exam. The highest possible score was 300, and I felt like a failure when I didn't score high enough to get into the program. Deep within myself, I knew that I had the ability to excel in every course in that program. I just needed a chance to prove myself. Fortunately, I was able to discuss the exam with the program director, who allowed me into the program on a provisional status. When I completed the first semester courses with As and Bs, I proved to myself that failures will not hinder my ability to accomplish any goals. I turned that particular failure into a window of opportunity.

However, you need to take specific steps to turn your own failures into windows of opportunity:

- First, accept the failure. Being honest with yourself about your failure is a tremendous milestone. Accepting the truth hurts, but it helps!

Second, evaluate the failure. Ask yourself what events in your life led to the failure. Did you make good choices or bad choices? Were your choices based on what you felt or what other people said about you? Did you have specific goals and a realistic action plan? These questions will help you evaluate why the failure occurred, which in turn will help you move forward and try again.

- Third, create an action plan to combat the failure. An action plan is a set of specific steps, based on realistic short- and long-term goals, that can lead to success. It includes details and a time frame for each goal.

The choice is yours. Allow your failures to become windows of opportunity, rather than obstacles that lead to defeat. Failures can build or deteriorate your character. Decide to use your failures as learning tools, not stumbling blocks!

## Pursuing Your Lost Dreams

While shopping at the mall for a birthday gift for her daddy, a little girl noticed that her favorite teddy bear had fallen out of her backpack. Afraid that someone had taken it, she asked her mother to help her look for it. Her mother overheard the little girl say to herself, "I won't lose hope or give up. I'll stay in this mall until I find my bear!" So the little girl searched for her bear in every store, looking under piles of clothing and checking into corners. Trying to persuade her to give up, her mother offered to buy the little girl another teddy bear. But the little girl said, "No, Momma, I want to find my teddy bear, and I won't stop looking for it." When they got to the food court, the little girl looked under every table and chair. Finally spotting her teddy bear, she leaped for joy and cried out, "Momma, I found my bear! I'm so glad that I didn't give up."

This is how we should pursue our lost dreams—with the same determination, courage, and perseverance displayed by this little girl searching for her lost teddy bear. Just as the little girl's mother encouraged her to stop searching, we have people in our lives who sometimes try to discourage us. They might cause us to doubt our potential or even try to persuade us to give up. But through her strong determination, the little girl was able to ignore her mom's discouraging words and *move forward*! She kept searching and didn't allow what others said to affect her drive to find her lost teddy bear. Likewise, we have to remain determined and committed to pursuing our dormant dreams and turning them into reality. Will this require hard work, dedication, and commitment? Yes, but it's worth it!

# Don't Be Afraid to Dream Big!

The little girl who lost her teddy bear displayed a courageous, confident attitude. Never be afraid to dream big, because fear will hinder your efforts. Never doubting your potential, pursue your dreams until they become reality. Serena and Venus Williams weren't afraid to dream big. Their parents saw the potential for these two young women to become phenomenal tennis players, and they challenged Serena and Venus to pursue their dreams. It required years of hard work, and at times they were probably afraid of falling short. Naysayers and doubters questioned whether the sisters had the talent and athleticism to climb all the way to the top in women's tennis. But Serena and Venus's undying belief in themselves caused their dreams to become reality.

Another big dreamer, Walt Disney, expressed his attitude about dreams in these words of wisdom: "All our dreams can come true, if we have the courage to pursue them." Disney's undying courage and determination overcame any fear and doubt that might have occasionally crossed his mind.

Everybody grows up with dreams and things that they want to accomplish in life. The difference is that some people make a strong commitment to pursue their dreams, but other people aren't willing to do that. Pursuing dreams requires action on your part. Your dream of becoming an orthodontist or an astronaut won't come true if you just sit around and do nothing. People have to take an active role in making their own dreams come true, which requires hard work, determination, commitment, self-discipline, courage, and self-confidence. Establish and activate a plan that will revitalize your dormant dreams! Proverbs 13:12 says, "Hope deferred makes the heart sick, but a dream fulfilled is a tree of life." What plans have you developed to achieve your dreams?

The fear of failure can be a strong deterrent. People sometimes worry that their talents and abilities might not be enough for them to achieve their dreams. Are you fearful of allowing yourself to dream? Discovering our dreams and goals requires us to do some soul searching and identify our fears, so that we can deal with them honestly. Writing books to help other people has always been one of my dreams, but first I had to do some soul searching. Fear and doubt tried to hinder me from pursuing this dream, but I courageously refused to allow Mr. Fear and Mrs. Doubt to stop me. With a determined belief in myself and my abilities, I designed an action plan to get this writing project completed, despite occasionally running into writer's block for a couple of days at a time. My inner determination sparked a strong desire to make this dream a reality!

Several steps helped me achieve my dream of writing this self-empowerment book for women. The first step is to clearly identify your dream and understand its connection to your purpose in life. Then you must recognize what it will take for you to achieve your dream and be willing to make any necessary sacrifice, especially since some dreams may be costly. It's also vitally important to possess an attitude of courage and commitment. As Langston James Hughes wrote,

"Hold fast to dreams, for if dreams die, life is a broken winged bird that cannot fly." Grasp your dreams tightly and never let fear crush them into oblivion. Stop making excuses and *dream big*!

**Words of Reflection:** The problem most people have is not dreaming big, but rather believing in themselves and having the courage to pursue what they really want to get out of life. —Walt Disney

# CHAPTER THREE

## Are You a Positive Risk Taker or a Watcher?

You gain strength, courage, and confidence by every experience in which you really stop to look fear in the face. The danger lies in refusing to face the fear, in not daring to come to grips with it. You must make yourself succeed every time. You must do the thing you think you cannot do.

—Eleanor Roosevelt

Although some people develop as risk takers, many people are born believing in the value of taking positive risks designed to develop their talents and abilities. For them, failure is neither an option nor an excuse. Several times in my life, I've taken positive risks. In 2000, after seven years as an elementary school teacher, I decided that I wanted to pursue a new career. After talking this over with my husband, I decided to enroll in the two-year master's of public administration program at Savannah State University. To pursue this goal, I was willing to take a tremendous salary cut, relinquish my nice summer vacations, and spend relentless days and nights studying.

I took this huge risk because I desired a change in my life—and I definitely got that change! Adjusting to graduate studies was a challenge because I hadn't attended college since 1990. I had to get used to attending evening classes, preparing presentations, and learning new course material such as administrative law and human resource management. I also got a part-time campus job as a graduate assistant in the MPA office, where I remained until graduation. I quickly learned that to be successful in the public administration program, I had to work twice as hard as my fellow students. Some days when I wanted to quit, I remembered the promise I made to myself to keep pushing forward and never give up. That kept me motivated and determined, and I graduated with honors in 2002.

## Characteristics of Positive Risk Takers

Roses have a unique smell, shape, and size that distinguish them from any other flower, just as positive risk takers have characteristics that make them different from other people. These men and women take risks that benefit them and their families without causing harm to other people. Positive risk takers exhibit self-confidence, perseverance, diligence, commitment, and determination. They view failure as an opportunity and challenge as a way to strengthen their character. They surround themselves with other risk takers and always speak positive words about themselves and others.

Positive risk takers are not afraid of failure. Mary Kay Ash, founder of Mary Kay Cosmetics, said, "When you reach an obstacle, turn it into an opportunity. You have the choice. You can overcome and be a winner, or you can allow it to overcome you and be a loser. The choice is yours and yours alone. Refuse to throw in the towel. Go that extra mile that failures refuse to travel. It is far better to be exhausted from success than to be rested from failure." Positive risk takers refuse to allow themselves to be governed by failure. Instead, they see failure as an opportunity to discover and experience their own strength, courage, and perseverance.

Positive risk takers also have a full tank of self-confidence, so that they are rarely bothered by disappointments, failures, and negative talk from others. Vincent Van Gogh, the famous nineteenth-century painter, said, "If you hear a voice within you say, you cannot paint, then by all means paint, and that voice will be silenced." Be confident in who you are, believe in yourself, and never listen to the voices of Mr. and Mrs. I Can't. If you don't believe in your talents, abilities, and potential, no one else will either. It all starts with *you*!

When you close your eyes and imagine your future, do you see success? Do you see yourself becoming a savvy entrepreneur or a top financial executive? How do you *see* yourself? Positive risk takers have an acute ability to visualize their own success. They believe in success, create realistic plans to reach success, and pursue it diligently. Phillis Wheatley (c. 1753–1784), the first published African American female poet, possessed the ability to visualize success for herself. Being born a slave didn't hinder her from accomplishing her goal of becoming a renowned poet and writer, because her vision of her own success was as bright and sharp as a two-edged sword.

As a young man, Abraham Lincoln went to war as a captain, returned as a private, and then failed as a businessman. He lost when he first ran for state legislature in 1832, and then lost again when he first ran for Congress in 1846. He was also defeated in his bid for the vice-presidential nomination at his party's national convention in 1856. Did he give up on his political ambitions? Absolutely not! He eventually became the sixteenth president of the United States of America, serving from 1861 to 1865.

Confucius said, "Our greatest glory is not in never falling but in rising every time we fall." Are you going to accept the challenge of being a positive risk taker? Take charge of your destiny and leap forward by taking positive risks. Smother those feelings of fear, doubt, and negative thinking that may be lurking deep within you.

## How Do I Become a Positive Risk Taker?

Sometimes taking a risk is a challenge even if it could benefit you and your family. For example, entering the MPA program after teaching for seven years was a difficult decision for me. But after examining the pros and cons, I made the decision to take a positive risk and pursue my professional goal of a new career. However, I had to take several steps to take that risk.

First, I needed a heart-felt desire to make a change in my life. I had become tired of the mundane rat race and wanted to pursue something different, but adapting to change wasn't easy. I had to design a realistic plan for making change happen in my life. Journeying through the change process required determination, courage, diligence, and self-confidence. Without these essential attributes, change would have never become a reality in my life. I had to maintain an attitude of determination, be courageous during tough times, exercise diligence to complete the MPA program, and maintain a high level of self-confidence. It was a challenge that I was willing to *meet*!

It's also vitally important to acknowledge and evaluate the risks that you're facing. As a positive risk taker, I had to examine the pros and cons of my decision. What are the positive benefits of taking a risk? Could it have a negative effect on the lives of other people? Do you have a realistic plan established before deciding to take the risk? Ask yourself these questions when becoming a positive risk taker.

Finally, it's essential to maintain a positive attitude. Catherine Pulsifer, the author of inspirational and motivational books, said, "A positive attitude is definitely one of the keys to success. My definition of a positive attitude is a simple one: looking for good in all circumstances." In my effort to maintain a positive attitude, it was important for me to focus on the benefits of transitioning to a new career. It would have been easy to let negative circumstances in my life shatter my goal of completing the MPA program. For example, my graduate assistantship was non - salaried and I had to attend classes year-round. But I refused to let negativity enter my heart and mind, which helped me maintain a positive attitude.

Accept the challenge of maintaining a positive attitude despite your circumstances. Bo Bennett, a renowned motivational speaker and businessman, said, "Having a positive mental attitude is asking how something can be done rather than saying it can't be done." Are you ready to become a positive risk taker and maintain a positive attitude? Be courageous and leap forward, because the sky is the limit!

## Are You a Watcher?

When you were a child, were there students in your class who seemed fearless? Some kids just bounce from one activity to another, always eager to be the first on the slide or monkey bars. These fearless students were also the first to offer an answer to a complex geometry problem, whether or not their answer was right. On the other hand, some of your childhood classmates and friends probably had to be pushed to try new things. They preferred to watch other students volunteer to spell a word for the teacher or be a team captain for kickball games at school. Why do some of us approach transitions and challenges with ease, while others find the same situations intimidating and scary?

Some people are risk watchers, rather than risk takers. Risk watchers observe other people taking positive risks, but they're afraid to take risks themselves. They have a watcher mentality because they watch other people achieve success, but they're afraid to leap forward and make success happen for themselves. They suffer from self-esteem issues that limit their confidence in their own talents and abilities.

Watchers are also fearful of their weaknesses, which overshadows their confidence in their strengths. For example, if you excel in science and struggle with geometry, then you're naturally going to focus on the strength of science, instead of finding out why geometry is a weakness. Understanding and accepting your weaknesses is essential when endeavoring to reach higher levels of success, because it helps you pinpoint the areas that need improvement. Time, energy, and hard work are then spent on turning those weaknesses into strengths, but that process requires commitment and perseverance.

Fear will also stifle your ability to accept and understand your weaknesses, but doing so will help you come to grips with areas that need improvement. Accepting your weaknesses is a sign of maturity, as you continue to grow and develop. Jean Vanier said, "Growth begins when we begin to accept our own weaknesses." What a profound statement of truth!

**Words of Reflection:** Don't be afraid to go out on a limb. That's where the fruit is. —H. Jackson Browne

# CHAPTER FOUR

# The Goal-Setter Attitude

"Setting goals is the first step in turning the invisible into the visible."
—Anthony Robbins

People are always setting goals for specific situations in their lives. Some people set goals for weight loss or regular exercise, while others set goals for saving money. When we set goals, we also need to plan how our goals will be accomplished. During my college years, I had to set goals for my career path and design a workable plan. I had to choose whether to become a nurse or a teacher, which was a tough decision because I had always wanted a career that allowed me to help others. Growing up, I had witnessed how my parents were dedicated to educating young children. My mother taught elementary students for thirty years. My father taught both elementary and high school students, but later in his career he developed a passion for adult education. After evaluating my options, I decided to pursue a degree in early elementary education.

It's unrealistic to think of journeying through life without having to make *any* decisions. After deciding to become an educator, my goal was to earn a bachelor of science degree in early elementary education. I decided to attend classes all year, rather than just August through May, knowing that I would need to stick to my plan and maintain a strong focus on completing the teacher education program. The program needed to be completed within four years, so I didn't have any time to waste. Being a young wife and mother of a newborn, I had to use my time wisely! Just like stocks are a valuable commodity for stockbrokers, time was my precious commodity. As Diana Scharf Hunt said, "Goals are dreams with deadlines."

# Becoming a Goal Setter

Goal setters are ambitious people who love to achieve success. Fitzhugh Dodson, a clinical psychologist who wrote numerous books about child rearing, profoundly states: "Without goals, and plans to reach them, you are like a ship that has set sail with no destination." Goal setters are self-motivated people who have a passion and commitment for change. As a new MPA graduate student, I had to set important goals for myself in the public administration program. The scope of information covered in a teacher education program includes early childhood development, effective teaching strategies, student assessment, and so on. However, a public administration program is much broader, providing core knowledge about topics such as human resource management, administrative law, and organizational culture. I had to establish realistic goals in order to successful complete the program.

As I began my journey into the MPA program, I set goals about which courses to take each semester, and I decided that I would graduate in 2002. To become a successful goal setter, I made a commitment to complete these simple steps:

- Know the goals that you want to accomplish. It is important to have an established idea about which goals you want to complete during a specified time period.
- List and prioritize your goals in a journal. If you don't write down your goals, you might lose them because it's more difficult to remain motivated.
- Establish a written time limit for each goal. Time limits help you stay focused and manage your time more wisely. If your goal is to lose twenty pounds within two months, for example, write that goal in your journal along with the time period in which it will be accomplished: "I will lose twenty pounds within two months."
- Design and write down a workable action plan. Action plans are useful because they provide a blueprint for *how* to accomplish your goals. Without the *how*, your goals become dead.
- Work the plan. Be active, not passive. Actions speak louder than words.

- Evaluate your action plan. Are your goals being accomplished within your specified time frame? Do you need more time to accomplish your goals?
- As each goal is completed, place a check mark by it and write down the date it was accomplished.

## Long-Term Goal Planning

Throughout your life journey, long-term goals allow you the opportunity to turn your dreams into reality. Possessing long-term goals can boost your quality of life by steering you into a positive pathway to success. How can you become a long-term goal planner? Begin with these three basic steps:

1. Focus your efforts on pursuing only one long-term goal at a time. Having too many goals at once will cause severe frustration and anxiety.
2. Set realistic goals and establish practical measures for accomplishing them. Realistic goals won't overwhelm you, and they can be achieved through hard work, diligence, and perseverance.
3. Persevere until the end. Perseverance must be embedded in you—no one can give it to

you, and it cannot be purchased from your local grocery store. If your goals are going to become a reality, you must have a pit bull mentality. When pit bulls attack their prey, their mindset is to never let go of the other animal. This is how you must be in life. No matter what obstacle you face, attack it and never let go of your goals.

Accept the challenge to become a long-term goal setter!

## Short-Term Goal Planning

Have you ever set a short-term goal to lose ten or fifteen pounds within a month? Do you remember designing a quick exercise plan to squeeze into a prom dress? Short-term goals require commitment. No matter how small the goal may seem, it still requires you to persevere and have an attitude of determination. Les Brown, a renowned motivational speaker, said, "Your goals are road maps that guide you and show you what is possible for your life." Imagine the possibilities and leap forward to accomplish your short-term goals. Grab fear by the neck and turn your goals into reality.

As a busy mother of three children, I used to frequently fall behind on doing our laundry. Even though I did laundry on Monday, dirty clothes would pile up again by Wednesday or Thursday, which was driving me *insane!* So I set a short-term goal of keeping up with the laundry. I decided that on Mondays I would wash *everything* in the baskets, but then I would wash one additional load of clothes *each day* to prevent them from piling up in our laundry room. Did this small goal require a level of commitment and determination? Yes, being consistent about washing a load of clothes each day was one of the keys to accomplishing this short-term goal.

Accomplishing your short-term goals will require you to be committed and dedicated, but there are also other helpful steps. One of the first things you should do is to start a short-term goal journal, because seeing your goals written on paper provides a visual prompt or stimulator. In your journal, write down all of your short-term goals. Start with the goal that most interests you, and then create a column for each of these areas:

- Steps that I can take right now to achieve this goal
- Steps that I can take next month
- Steps that I can take in six months
- Obstacles that could prevent me from achieving this goal
- Thoughts about my ability to complete this goal

For example, if your short-term goal is to save money for a summer vacation, write this goal at the top of your paper. Then list five things that you can do right now to save money for your summer vacation, such as packing your lunch each day, spending less money on extracurricular activities, using coupons, getting a cheaper cell phone plan, or purchasing clothing only during the off season. Set a specific completion deadline, which will help you stay on track and not procrastinate. When the goal has been completed, place a checkmark next to it.

Short-term goal planning can be a rewarding experience. Maintaining a positive attitude coupled with determination, commitment, and dedication will make your short-term goals a reality. Don't be afraid of the challenge to become a short-term goal planner!

**Words of Reflection:** Our goals can only be reached through a vehicle of a plan, in which we must fervently believe, and upon which we must vigorously act. There is no other route to success. —Stephen A. Brennan

# CHAPTER FIVE

# Where are your Standards?

"The quality of a leader is reflected in the standards they set for themselves."
—Ray Kroc

Have you ever wondered why some women set higher standards for themselves than others? Have you had to evaluate some standards in your life? What type of standards do you possess? These questions are useful in understanding the importance of establishing high standards for yourself. Standards aren't what you think you should do or what you think other people want or expect you to do. Rather, standards are behaviors that you commit to because they set the stage for how you govern yourself. Setting higher or lower standards affects the level of expectations that you have for yourself.

Ladies, if you have low expectations for yourself, you'll receive little results. If you have high expectations, you'll receive big results. The choice is yours. Establishing higher standards for yourself will stretch your potential and keep you from thinking of yourself as mediocre. Many women are satisfied with being mediocre, which requires no effort on their part. The *real* challenge lies in consistently demanding more of yourself and establishing a new level of commitment to be the best at whatever you endeavor to do in life.

Let's take a look at an influential woman who set high standards and demanded more of herself. Mae Jemison was born in Decatur, Alabama, on October 17, 1956. In 1988, upon completing the astronaut training program, Dr. Jemison became the first black female astronaut. On September 12, 1992, she became the first African-American woman to go into space. By emulating successful women such as Jemison, we too can set high standards, demand more of ourselves, and accomplish great things.

Setting higher standards is also an essential part of how women build relationships with men. For many years our diminished standards have negatively affected how we present ourselves to men and reinforced the stereotype that every woman is desperate for a man. Let's change this stereotype and prove to the world that we are special creations who deserve to be treated with the utmost respect, dignity, and gentleness. Be courageous, set your standards high, and refuse to accept less. If you expect your companion to open the door for you on date night, maintain that standard and don't accept anything less. If you expect your companion to pull out your chair for you at the dinner table, maintain that standard. If you expect roses or special gifts for your birthday, maintain that standard. If you expect complete honesty in your relationship, maintain that standard. Whatever your standards are, be bold enough to *maintain* them and expect nothing less. Men will sit back and observe whether or not *you* maintain your standards. It's practical thinking—if you set high standards and expect nothing, you receive nothing. If you set high standards and expect much, your companion will live up to your standards.

## What Are You Demanding of Yourself?

Isn't it time to challenge yourself to be the best? Start demanding more of yourself than mediocrity. Destroy your excuses and leap forward to be a woman of greatness, determination, perseverance, strength, and hope. Decide for yourself that you are worthy of dignity, love, respect, and honor.

Do you feel cozy and relaxed in your comfort zone? We all have these safe havens, whether it's our job seniority or the complacency of living in the same city for twenty years. These comfort zones prevent us from pushing ourselves to be better, brighter, and sharper! Pushing beyond our comfort zones makes us more stronger and determined people.

I had to get out of my comfort zone and demand more of myself when I started a new weight-lifting program. I've always been small-framed and never had any problems maintaining my weight, but I wanted to tone up my entire body—legs, arms, abs, and buttocks. As we get older, metabolism slows down and we might not be as toned as during our teen years or those terrific twenties. After giving birth to three beautiful daughters, I wanted a hard body again, so I endeavored to make it happen. My loving husband encouraged me to join him in a weight-lifting program to lose fat.

First, I had to make a genuine commitment to stick with the exercise plan. My husband could not make that commitment for me—I had to resolve for myself to do the exercise plan four times a week. I put specific demands on myself such as being consistent and trying heavier weights, which wasn't easy. Some days I would feel so nauseated because of the extreme intensity of lifting heavier weights or performing more reps, but I knew that this was all just part of the commitment.

In the process, I learned a valuable lesson. Placing demands on yourself requires you to stretch beyond your previous limits and stop making excuses for why you can't do something. It requires you to look deep within yourself and pull out the best. It requires an undying commitment to making a change in your life. Lastly, it requires determination to be better today than yesterday—and better tomorrow than today! One of my favorite poems talks about how we should take the challenge to put demands on ourselves and never quit. Read this poem and meditate on what it means to you:

Don't Quit

When things go wrong, as they sometimes will,
When the road you're trudging seems all uphill,
When funds are low and the debts are high,
And you want to smile, but you have to sigh,
When care is pressing you down a bit,
Rest if you must, but don't you quit.

Life is queer with its twists and turns,
As every one of us sometimes learns,
And many a failure turns about
When he might have won had he stuck it out.

Don't give up though the pace seems slow,
You may succeed with another blow …

Success is failure turned inside out,
The silver lining of the clouds of doubt
And you never can tell how close you are—
It may be near when it seems so far.
So stick to the fight when you're hardest hit,
It's when things seem worst that you mustn't quit …

Putting demands on yourself challenges you to push beyond your normal limits and adopt a non-quitting attitude. Demand excellence and determination from yourself, more and more every day. Take simple steps to become a better person. Demand of yourself that you will be punctual, speak positively, and live with integrity. Pursue your dreams and goals, smiling right through the tough times. Demand the best of yourself. Take a leap forward to stretch beyond your comfort zone and dive into the challenge zone!

**Words of Reflection:** The life of a high achiever is one of risk and reward, one of sowing and reaping, and/or one of straining and growing. Nothing great will happen unless you first take a risk, sow the right seed, and/or strain through resistance. Get started and make your dreams come true. —Greg Warner

# CHAPTER SIX

# Woman, Where's Your Self-Confidence?

The way to develop self-confidence is to do the thing you fear.

—William Jennings Bryan

Life is full of disappointment and tough times, and sometimes we feel like we just can't do anything right. When we allow our failures to destroy our self-confidence, it's difficult to envision success for ourselves. Life becomes a never-ending rat race, a daily chore that we drag ourselves through with our heads hanging low. We wake up, wash our faces, brush our teeth, get dressed, deliver the children to school, and go to work—without the confidence to tackle any obstacles or challenges.

But I'm challenging you to pick yourself up, hold your beautiful head high, and *leap* forward into your purpose. Failure is *never* an option. Your only option is to get past your failures and design a plan to reach success. I'm challenging you to get your self-confidence back and realize that you were created for *greatness*!

Two caterpillars were faced with the task of crawling up a steep hill. Nothing was too hard for Alexandria, whose courage and self-confidence were inspiring to her fellow caterpillars. Victoria, however, was fearful and lacked self-confidence, which made her apprehensive about trying new challenges. She had always heard others say that she didn't have enough strength or tenacity to climb steep hills, and she had come to believe them. Alexandria and Victoria had been best friends for a long time, and one day they met at the bottom of the hill.

Always looking for a challenge, Alexandria told herself, *I can make it up this hill. I won't quit. I'm confident in myself.* Then she turned to Victoria and said, "Let's see who can reach the top of this hill first." "Well, I'll try," replied Victoria, "but I might not make it. I don't have enough strength to crawl that far." She was thinking, *I'm tired and I can't crawl to the top of this steep hill. I just don't have enough self-confidence.*

Alexandria kept crawling upward until she reached the top of the hill. Then she looked down at Victoria, still close to the bottom of the hill, and yelled, "Where's your self-confidence? You can do it. Keep trying. Don't give up." Victoria heard her friend's words of encouragement, but she couldn't find the strength to crawl up the hill. She yelled back to Alexandria, "This hill is too high for me. I'm quitting. It's just too hard!" Alexandria just looked down at Victoria and wondered what had happened to her self-confidence.

This story represents a common scenario. Some people won't allow any difficulties to shatter their self-confidence. They press on through their challenges and reach for success. "I quit" is simply not in their vocabulary. Other people throw in the towel when they encounter obstacles. Their self-confidence dwindles and success seems out of reach. In the words of Samuel

Johnson, "Self-confidence is the first requisite to great undertakings."

What great undertakings do you face that require you to press on despite challenges? Alexandria made it to the top of the hill because she was confident and unafraid. She looked past the difficulty and pressed on toward her goal. But Victoria allowed fear and criticism from others to undermine her self-confidence. Alexandria was driven by courage, whereas Victoria was driven by fear and doubt. What will be the driving force in your life?

Maybe you once possessed great self-confidence, but somewhere along the way you began to doubt your ability to accomplish your goals. Maybe you're wondering, *Where is my self-confidence, how did I lose it, and how can I get it back?* Sometimes we allow tough times to steal our self-confidence. For example, when other people reject us for some reason, it can shatter our self-confidence and cause us to experience low self-esteem. The key is to accept your special talents and abilities and not allow rejection from other people to hinder you from accomplishing your goals. Major disappointments, such as unemployment, divorce, or financial problems, also can shatter our self-confidence and make us feel like life isn't worth living. But you can choose not to allow these hindrances to stop you from dreaming and pursuing your goals.

## Keys to Developing Your Self-Confidence

Self-confidence is one of the most essential qualities for success. When you are confident, you believe in your abilities to accomplish your goals. You're not intimidated by others, and you don't make excuses for *not* doing your best. There are three important steps to developing self-confidence and feeling energized to pursue your goals:

1.    Change your way of thinking. Imagine your mind as a garden where the thoughts that you plant can yield a harvest of good or bad fruit. Make sure that you plant good thoughts in your mind. I love this quotation by Benjamin Disraeli: "[Everyone] should nurture their

minds with great thoughts, for you will never go any higher than you think."

2. Accept yourself. One of life's greatest challenges is to recognize that you are imperfect and uniquely different from anyone else. However, don't let the fact that you aren't perfect be an excuse for not being or doing your best. Instead, ask yourself every day what you're doing to make yourself a better person. If you have the God-given talent to organize events, then do it! If you're able to put together beautiful floral arrangements, then do it!

3. Surround yourself with positive role models and self-confident people. I didn't really understand the meaning of "Birds of a feather flock together" until I became an older adult. My parents, husband, and friends are great mentors and positive role models, and I've learned from their successes and been inspired by them to do my best in all my endeavors.

It is vitally important to develop self-confidence, and nobody else can do it for you. Now is the time to accept responsibility for cultivating your self-confidence and become a go-getter! Ponder these words of Sir Edmund Hillary: "It is not the mountain we conquer, but ourselves." The real challenge is not overcoming obstacles in life, but conquering our own negative thinking and feelings of low self-esteem. That's the *real* challenge!

## Maintaining Your Self-Confidence

Body builders work hard to get in superb shape by developing muscle mass and strength, but it's also important to maintain a low percentage of body fat. Acquiring the muscles and strength is a task, but *maintaining* it requires a whole new level of commitment and dedication. Similarly, even though we take steps to develop our self-confidence, it's also imperative that we maintain it, which requires a commitment to thinking positively about ourselves, surrounding ourselves with positive role models, and learning about success from other self-confident people.

It's time to take control of your self-confidence and maintain that belief in yourself. Just like it takes hard work and commitment to maintain a good marriage or a healthy physique, it requires energy and tenacity to maintain your self-confidence. In my readings, I stumbled across these thought-provoking words by Marcus Garvey: "If you have no confidence in self, you are twice defeated in the race of life. With confidence, you have won even before you have started." This quotation reminded me how essential it is for us to develop and maintain our self-confidence.

It takes commitment and dedication to maintain belief in ourselves. However, there are a few specific keys that will help you sustain that good feeling about who you are and what you can accomplish. As I look back on my life, I see how these key points helped me through discouraging and tough times. As a young mother and wife at eighteen years old, sometimes I felt that the challenges I faced were insurmountable. I had to learn how to endure and persevere when I didn't have enough money for college, or when I wanted to drop out because it was too difficult to juggle the responsibility of being a mother and wife. I really had to pull confidence from deep within to help me through those challenging times.

The first thing I had to do was not get discouraged and allow my setbacks to determine my destiny. Setbacks are just opportunities to see what you're really made of when the tough times come your way. Are you made of sand or rocks? Sand washes away when the raging storms come, but rocks remain steady and strong. I had to stand strong as a rock when there wasn't enough money for my college tuition, when we didn't have a car to take me to campus, and when I just wanted to give up.

The next key to maintaining my self-confidence was to appreciate and value my accomplishments and achievements. At various times in my life, I've needed to remind myself of the goals that I've accomplished— graduating from high school with honors, earning a bachelor of science degree in early elementary education, raising my children, and finishing graduate school with a master's degree in public administration. Never forget what you've accomplished, because it helps you press forward toward other goals and dreams.

Finally, I had to acknowledge my fears. This was the most challenging thing to do because it required me to ask myself these questions: Am I fearful of failing? Am I fearful of new challenges? Am I confident in my talents and abilities? The Word of God instructs us in 2 Timothy 1:7, "That God has not given us a spirit of fear and timidity, but of power, love, and self-discipline." Fear can become a prison, keeping you from accomplishing the dreams that God has placed in your heart. Release your fear and take hold of your dreams!

In your lifetime, you will face many challenges, disappointments, setbacks, and fears. But the choice is yours to build and maintain that self-confidence that is hidden deep inside you. It's not easy to bounce back from your setbacks, smile through your disappointments, and overcome your fears. But one thing is for sure—it's always possible to do the impossible! Philippians 4:13 encourages us to understand that "I can do all things through Christ who gives me strength." Believe in your talents and abilities. Believe in that determination and courage that lies inside of you. Just believe. Only believe.

**Words of Reflection:** Don't live down to expectations. Go out there and do something remarkable. —Wendy Wasserstein

# CHAPTER SEVEN

## What Happened to my Character Nuggets?

Be more concerned with your character than your reputation. Your character is what you really are while your reputation is merely what others think you are.
—John Wooden

Is your trustworthiness collecting dust on a shelf? Has your honesty diminished? These aspects of your character are vitally important because they define you. How beautiful you are on the outside isn't nearly as important as your inner character radiating outward, showing people that you are trustworthy, responsible, a dedicated citizen of your community, caring, and honest. Outward beauty fades over time, but these inner qualities can remain vibrate and alive.

When you hear the word *character*, what comes to your mind? Do you see someone who is caring and empathetic, trustworthy and loyal? Someone who shows respect to others? Character is simply who you are. Your success and happiness depend on who you are, not on your material possessions or how you look on the outside. Your character matters, and it's up to you to develop these essential attributes of respect, trustworthiness, responsibility, fairness, caring, and citizenship. Will you accept the challenge to nurture and build your character?

As an elementary school teacher, I taught many children who came from poor and middle-class families. One little girl always came to school without any barrettes or ribbons in her uncombed hair, and yet she was enthusiastic and passionate about learning. Moved by compassion, I decided to buy some accessories to make her hair look nice. I was happy to do something special for her. I didn't want any accolades or recognition—my only desire was to be a blessing to that precious child. I could have turned my head and acted as though I didn't care about her appearance, but my character radiated with an unselfish, caring attitude toward my student. Don't be afraid to develop your character and grow into that beautiful woman that you were destined to be!

## Character Development

Some people spend their time training to run marathons, and others devote quality time to developing their businesses and generating income. But how many people do you know actually invest quality time in developing their character? Character development is an active process of molding yourself into a person who is trustworthy, responsible, fair, caring, and respectful, and displays good citizenship. However, without hard work, dedication, and commitment, you won't witness any changes in your character. J. B. Gough sheds light on a solid truth: "Reputation is for time; character is for eternity."

Three important steps will help you develop your character. Remember that character is what defines you, so take the time to develop honesty, trustworthiness, and a caring attitude toward others. Developing your character will benefit you and others around you. Throughout my life, I've used these three character development tips to help me become a woman of good character.

The first step is to acknowledge that you want to change. If you're tired of being a dishonest person, make a genuine commitment to be honest. Only you can make that change. With each situation that arises, make a conscious decision to be an honest person. If you never acknowledge that fact that you want to change, your negative character traits, such as dishonesty, irresponsibility, and an uncaring attitude, will remain dominant in your life.

Secondly, work on your character daily. Every day poses an opportunity to show your good character. Daily experiences will allow you to exhibit trustworthiness, honesty, respectfulness, and a caring attitude. Find a meaningful way each day to display your good character. I've come to realize that working on my character takes hard work, commitment, dedication, determination, and a willingness to change!

Finally, surround yourself with people who display good character. As the old saying goes, "Birds of a feather flock together." It's important to watch your associations and friendships. When I was teaching, I noticed how some well-behaved students would begin to misbehave and their attitudes would deteriorate when they became friends with other students who were unruly. Parents would often be shocked when I met with them to discuss their children's changed behavior, because their children would behave at home where they weren't around their unruly friends.

Because other people can influence your behavior, it's important to evaluate the character of your friends and associations. As the saying goes, "Bad associations corrupt good manners." The people with whom you surround yourself can influence your decision making and adversely affect how you pursue your goals. Make a genuine effort to surround yourself with people who reflect the kind of person you desire to be. Always remember that a person's behavior is more important than their words, appearance, education, and socioeconomic status. Develop friendships with people who can help make you a better person. Distinguished leadership author John Maxwell teaches a valuable principle: "A leader's potential is determined by those closest to him." Make a wise choice to surround yourself with people who have good character, dreams, goals, and a passion to be their *best*!

**Words of Reflection:** Good character is more to be praised than outstanding talent. Most talents are, to some extent a gift. Good character, by contrast, is not given to us. We have to build it, piece by piece—by thought, choice, courage, and determination.

—H. Jackson Brown

# EPILOGUE

## TRUE BEAUTY FROM WITHIN

Why did I take the time to write this book? It's simple. I wanted to encourage women of all races, ethnicities, and economic backgrounds to understand that they are *more than pretty faces*! We are more than beautiful hair, soft lips, and nice, slender legs. Our true beauty resides on the inside of us. God has created us to be confident, strong, courageous, intelligent, creative, witty, articulate, honest, trustworthy, responsible, caring, persistent, and full of determination! *More Than a Pretty Face* was written to help women value their inner beauty, regain their self-confidence, and pursue those lost dreams. I hope this book inspires you to set goals and standards for your life. My desire is that you begin to see yourself as a successful woman who is destined for greatness and created for a purpose. Accept the challenge to be *more than a pretty face*!

For More Than a Pretty Face Empowerment Seminars, workshops, vision-board sessions, and motivational speaking engagements, contact me:

LaShone L. Grimes
P.O Box 61633
Savannah, GA 31419
Email: lgrimes.hhl@gmail.com
Office: (912) 547-7385

# NOTES

1. www.invitinghome.com
2. www.brucevanhorn.com
3. www.sapphhr.net
4. www.passiton.com
5. www.3canisius.edu
6. www.ekrfoundation.org
7. www.gurteen.com
8. https://insearchofheroes.com
9. https://frugalentrepreneur.com
10. www.wloe.org
11. https://brightdrops.com
12. www.BibleGateway.com
13. https://m.poets.org
14. www.keepinspiring.me
15. www.goodreads.com
16. www.marykaytribute.com
17. www.brainyquote.com
18. www.poetryfoundation.org
19. https://en.m.wikipedia.org
20. www.quoteinvestigator.com
21. www.azquotes.com
22. www.thinkexist.com

23. www.thequotablecoach.com
24. www.quotecatalog.com
25. https://beleaderly.com
26. www.allauthor.com
27. https://quotefancy.com
28. www.7rulesofachievement.com
29. www.space.com
30. www.yourdailypoem.com
31. https://www.medioq.com
32. www.quotes.net
33. https://quotationcelebration.wordpress.com
34. https://en.m.wikiquote.org
35. https://keyamsha.com
36. www.bestsayingquotes.com
37. www.BibleGateway.com
38. https://m.bayt.com
39. www.jesseneo.com
40. www.thedailyhatch.org
41. https://theleaderslocker.com
42. https://izquotes.com

# ABOUT THE AUTHOR

LaShone Grimes is a native of Savannah, Georgia. She attended Armstrong State University and earned a bachelor of science degree in early elementary education. After teaching in the Chatham County Public School System for seven years, she earned a master's degree in public administration from Savannah State University. After graduate school, she served as executive director of Urban Hope, a nonprofit organization that provided after-school program services for elementary, middle, and high school students. At Urban Hope, she collaborated with churches and schools to provide tutoring and mentoring services for students. High school students earned community service hours at the after-school program and became "reading buddies" with elementary children.

LaShone became the First Lady of Maranatha Church International in 2010. Pastor Wayne Grimes and LaShone are diligently fulfilling the divine purpose of their lives by teaching others how to follow the plan that God has for their lives. The vision at Maranatha is to "build faith, embrace, elevate, transform, and equip lives from the inside out to further the Kingdom of God." Additionally, LaShone is passionate about building self-esteem and courage in girls and women. Her mission is to help young ladies to recognize that true beauty radiates from within. She is the creator and the facilitator of "More Than a Pretty Face" workshops and empowerment sessions for young ladies in the city of Savannah. Through the More Than a Pretty Face program, she has mentored and empowered hundreds of girls. *More Than a Pretty Face* will empower young women to value and love their inner beauty. LaShone's belief is that we are created to be strong vessels of courage, determination, perseverance, and self-confidence.

LaShone has been married to Wayne Grimes for twenty-eight years and is the proud mother of three amazing daughters. She also has three precious grandchildren. Additionally, LaShone is an active member of the Hilton Head (SC) Chapter of the Links, Incorporated. During her spare time, she enjoys traveling, reading, Zumba, and spending time with family.

# ABOUT THE BOOK

Women's self-esteem can sometimes be shattered by failures, disappointments, and difficult times. However, we can regain self-esteem by believing in ourselves and valuing our beautiful inner qualities such as determination, courage, self-confidence, and perseverance. *More Than a Pretty Face* will provide women with a renewed appreciation of their unique, individual qualities. Allow God to transform your mindset and bring you to a peaceful place of realizing your worth! This life-changing journey of empowerment will ignite a passion within women to recognize that they are created for greatness and designed for a special purpose. Find out how you can dream big beyond the ordinary and value your precious inner beauty.

Printed in the United States
By Bookmasters